Windows into the Soul

WINDOWS INTO THE SOUL

POEMS OF TRAVEL AND REFLECTION

Lauren "Buzz" Yoder

Faraway Publishing
Black Mountain, N.C.

Copyright © 2026 by Lauren "Buzz" Yoder
All rights reserved. First Edition

The author may be contacted at
41 Wagon Trail
Black Mountain, NC 28711
laurenw.yoder@gmail.com

Published by
FARAWAY PUBLISHING
125 Spring View Drive
Black Mountain, N.C. 28711
farawaypublishing@gmail.com

Faraway Publishing values copyright protection, which plays a crucial role in inspiring creativity, encouraging diverse narratives, supporting free speech, and promoting a vibrant culture. Thank you for purchasing an officially authorized edition of this book and for complying with copyright laws by not reproducing, scanning, or distributing any part of it in any form without permission. Your support helps our authors and enables Faraway Publishing to continue publishing books for all types of readers.

ISBN-13: 979-8-9990731-3-6 (pbk.)
Library of Congress Control Number: 2026933141

Printed in the United States of America
10 9 8 7 6 5 4 3 2 1

Cover Image: A window in the Château de Chenonceau overlooking the Cher River. Cover design by Brian Wilson
All photographs by Lauren Yoder

*Ce grand monde, c'est le miroir où il nous
faut regarder pour nous connaître de bon biais.*
— Michel de Montaigne

This great world is the mirror
into which we must look
to truly know ourselves.

*Il faut voyager pour frotter et limer
sa cervelle contre celle d'autrui.*
— Michel de Montaigne

We must travel in order
to rub and polish
our wit
against that of others.

CONTENTS

Preface xi
Acknowledgments xiii
Awaken 1
Ecliptic Thoughts, April '24 2
Lascaux Eclipse 4
Mockingbird's Eclipse 6
17th of Germinal 7
Red-winged blackbird 8
When Days Seem Gray 9
April Art 10
Caminando 11
Kafumba 12
Old Grist Mill Wheel 14
Nature's Fireworks 16
Moon Over Gaza 18
Dream Paths 19
Fruit Bats 20
Haikus Inspired by Ring Lake 22
Regrets? 23
Night Sounds 24
Wind in Our Valley 26
Inspiration on the Beach 28
"The More Things Change" 29
Desert Monsoon 30
Hummingbird in Rain 32
Come Walk With Me 34
Cultivate your garden 35
Celebration in Times of Conflict 36
Sourwood Soliloquy 37
Heron Tears 38
Beaver in Storm 40
Land Mine 42
Grenade at Night 43

Hidden Life in Bleak Midwinter	44
Mulling	45
Rub a Dub	46
Edelweiss	47
Erosion	48
Mutuality	49
Walking, Walking	50
The Happiness Quotient	51
Blueberry Gratitude	52
Nuit de Saint Jean	53
Discovering Red Shirt Lake	54
Osprey at Ring Lake	56
Nature's Bounty	57
Friendly Flames	58
Beginning	59
Night Thoughts	60
Red-tailed Hawk	61
Hobo, Eight Years Old	62
Heron Fishermen	64
Nature's Lesson	65
Parisian Cobblestones	66
Melancholy Moon	68
Pyramidal Beauty	70
Lucky Thirteen	71
New Castle	72
White Gold?	74
In Gothic Chapel	76
Alsatian Spring	77
My Vineyard, My Heritage	78
The Joy of Sidewalk Cafés	80
Golden Magic	81
Pick-up-sticks	82
Ode to Water Power	83
Market Seasons	84

Paris Street Urchin	86
Storks Are Back!	88
Bread	89
Marauders	90
Hunger in Gaza	92
Hands	93
Pilgrim Stream	94
Summer Night Sounds	95
First Rain	96
Summer's End	98
Tropical Night	100
Camino Welcome	102
Toward Nothingness	103
Powerless	104
Cold August Wind	106
Baby Beluga Lament	107
Anticipation	108
Rivers	109
Bristlecone Pine	110
Peaceful Rivers	111
Morning Bliss	112
Mining Claim	114
Resilience	115
Seed of the Universe	116
Softness	117
Gray Fall Morning	118
Disappearing Mountains	119
A November Blessing	120
Winter Forest Bathing	122
Trash Day	124
Changing Nature	126
Winter Wonder	127
A Cyclist's Obituary	128
Culinary Surprise	130

Cherry Tree at Window 131
Arrival 132
Soupe à l'oignon 133
A Spring Blessing 134
Endurance 135
Lucky Luke 136

PREFACE

Traveling has always offered me the opportunity to open windows into other cultures and at the same time to measure myself and rethink my own beliefs and opinions. Ordinary life at home is good and meaningful, but traveling and especially living in other settings encourages me to open my eyes to new beauties, to experience unusual situations, and learn from the unexpected comments of those who confront different realities, even as they share the same human values of honesty, hospitality, kindness, and love for family and country. Furthermore, I can delight in nature's varied magnificence: from the red deserts of the American Southwest to the rolling, green hills and luxurious tropical forests of Central Africa or floral abundance of blue wisteria draped over gray stone façades in narrow cobblestoned French villages.

Reflecting on my experiences in verse gives permanence to those experiences, allowing me to savor them again and again and to consider how their reflection has enriched my life.

I trust that these glimpses into nature and human interactions allow readers to open windows into their own comparable experiences and to reflect on how those windows can become mirrors in which they, too, can see themselves more clearly.

Lauren Yoder
Black Mountain, NC
February, 2026

ACKNOWLEDGMENTS

For the love of travel and of reading, I thank my father who was always dreaming of another trip and who frequently, after my begging, would surprise me with a book that would open up distant and exotic worlds, sparking my imagination. And I remember that my mother delighted in reciting poems she had memorized, encouraging me to do likewise, though I never reached her level of proficiency. I owe a debt of gratitude as well to sisters who loved to play school. It was in those makeshift classrooms that I composed my first poems, and fortunately none have survived.

I am most grateful to my wife, Sydney, for her constant support, for her acceptance of the stacks of poetry books that sometimes clutter our coffee table and risk collapsing off my desktop and bookshelves.

I continue to appreciate the friends in our monthly poetry group, for the poems they bring are always a reminder of the beauty of words and their power to awaken emotions.

Brian Wilson generously proposed the initial design for the cover to include the adapted photograph of the château window. For that I thank him.

My sincerest thanks must go to Ran Shaffner, my editor and publisher, whose keen eye, mastery of language, skill with layout, patience, and unlimited energy conspire to turn dross into something closer to gold. I prize his friendship.

AWAKEN

When the morning fog hangs low over the mountains,
and night has triggered fearful dreams,
or radio waves twist with hate,
When routine covers all with iron chains,
When lies buzz in ears like fearsome yellowjackets,
When even favorite foods have lost their savor,
When the future fills with tornado clouds,
When life itself risks losing meaning,

Lift a magnifier to the tiny,
to the pattern on the white oak leaf,
to the multicolored heart of blue cohosh flower,
flame azalea's orange glow.
And raise your eyes at night
when the moon is hidden
to consider, with spyglass if you can,
Big Dipper spinning round North Star,
chasing pain of darkest dreams.

As the morning greets you,
allow your mind to capture spring's perfumes,
scented lilac, heady multiflora rose,
and look into the eyes of friendship
sparkling with love's support.

ECLIPTIC THOUGHTS, APRIL '24

I. **In the Indiana cemetery,**
old gray tombstones stood slanted,
covered with moss,
deep green in the darkening sky.

In the woods nearby,
as the sun awoke
from behind the moon,
the white fawn lily raised its head.

II. **The facts lie hidden**
like diurnal planets
behind the politician's
rambling words.

But when an active mind
blacks out the cant,
the naked truth appears
like Venus when moon hides sun.

III. **The moon slips slowly 'cross**
the sun's bright face.
The birds go quietly
and drop into the spruce to roost.

A slice of light appears
and the avian chorus erupts
as the new sun dawns
in early afternoon.

IV. **Ancestors gazed in wonder**
   as the sun disappeared at noon
   and the planets shone brightly,
   high and clear in midday sky.

   I too gaze in wonder
   that in precision wise ones can predict
   that sun and moon today
   conjoin once more with earth.

V. **You hold the cardboard steady**
   as centered pinhole perforation
   on white surface spread below
   projects bright thin crescent sun.

   As camera obscura projects true image
   so too I feel the reassuring warmth
   of radiating heartfelt love
   deep within my welcoming soul.

LASCAUX ECLIPSE

Today I slipped into my Lascaux cave
with my precious ochre paints:
orange, red, and yellow. On the wall,
with charcoal outline first, I sketched
our family totem, sacred horse.

When I pulled myself back through
the hidden opening
into the morning air,
the birds had paused their singing
and a cool breeze swept over me.

I glanced up,
and suddenly I noticed
that a slice of sun
had disappeared,
a small bite taken
at upper edge.

As I started home
through hillside thyme,
I looked again in fright,
and half the sun was gone,
our source of warmth and wealth.

I began to tremble, mouth dry.
Some spirit, more powerful than our sun,
perhaps was raging
because in jest the horse I drew
was cowardly yellow and not heroic red.

My eyes now burned, but quaking,
in deep awe I looked again
and saw that now our sun
was mere crescent in the sky,
about to leave our world in darkness.

I hugged my ochre paints, especially red,
and slipped back through the opening.
My oil lamp lit, I overlaid the ugly yellow
with vibrant red, and as I left the cave,
the painted horse snorted firm approval.

The sun was almost full again.
The birds once more began to sing.
As I clutched my precious ochre paints,
my soul rejoiced in gratitude
for the deep and wondrous power of paint.

MOCKINGBIRD'S ECLIPSE

When the eclipse starts, they said,
the birds fall silent.

But today, as darkened moon
began to overlay the sun,
instead of seeking roost
like other songbirds
in neighboring oak and cedar
and like the chickens
that stopped their scratching
to walk the ramp as for nightly rest,
the mockingbird flew to tip of highest spruce.

Like his summer midnight serenades
in honeysuckle-perfumed air
as song and scent poured through my open window,
this day he launched into his varied repertoire,
mimicking titmouse, jay and sparrow,
creating anthems to the hidden sun,
filling cooling air and dusk-like darkness
for full four minutes till lunar disk
relinquished mastery and daytime light returned.

17TH OF GERMINAL

Amid wildflowers, April birdsong,
And budding green displays,
With germinating love
Our troth we pledged
Midst dearest friends.
As April's flowers bloom once more,
And birds resume their serenade,
I gaze into your blue-green eyes
And breathe deep gratitude
For loving presence by my side,
Adding spice to life,
Demonstrating creativity,
Seeking, finding beauty,
And encouraging integrity.

RED-WINGED BLACKBIRD

A black bird perches by water's edge
on cattail tall or on small maple tree
whose newest leaves shine red in sun.
Then, I watch, as wings aflutter, he rises
into the wind, red-orange epaulets
flashing to display his strength.

His energy's a model
for all the world to see.
He always shares his qualities—
his penetrating song,
his brilliant colors,
and his confidence supreme.

When the red-winged blackbird
spreads his wings and rises on the wind,
with shoulder patches blazing orange, red,
he teaches all to display true colors,
bringing joy, inspiring creativity,
and sharing with the world.

WHEN DAYS SEEM GRAY

When days seem gray,
    lie on your back and watch the clouds
    open a bag of dark chocolate
    imagine flying with the crows

When days seem gray,
    walk barefoot on the grass
    savor a pot of tea
    place a seed in potting soil

When days seem gray,
    watch an old movie once again
    name your own constellation in the night sky
    smile at a stranger

When days seem gray,
    feel your voice box vibrate as you hum a tune
    consider the Big Bang
    slap abstract color on canvas

When days seem gray,
    climb a tall tree in your mind
    practice speaking dog or cat
    caress velvet 'tween thumb and finger

When days seem gray,
    smile in surprise at the dear face in the mirror
    open inner eye to memory of loved ones lost
    and always live in gratitude for tiny things.

APRIL ART

The artist stands tall at tableside.
She picks up a shallow box,
perhaps the cherry wood with deep red grains,
perhaps black walnut glowing amber,
or even glossy spalted maple.

Next she reaches for textured paper,
handmade with love
from old fabric, wool, or cotton,
or paper mulberry bark,
some pastel blue, some walnut brown.

Then nimble fingers form
from Gelli printed paper
or photographic colors
pyramids both large and small
in graceful origami folds.

To link the forms and textures,
richly colored yarns, she twists and turns.
Their loops and knots
untie the varied shapes and colors,
creating a brand-new world of beauty.

With the ritual, linking tints and forms,
the artist commemorates
the April union once more renewed
of human gifts and spirits,
portrayal of a solid universe of love.

CAMINANDO

Staff in hand, water flask over shoulder,
broad hat protects me from harsh meseta sun.
I push fatigue to deep recesses of my mind,
stretching limbs toward Santiago.

One foot forward, then the other,
muscle memory replaying myriad joys
of early walk, matching stride with son
through green Galician hills.

Reliving sips of crisp Albariño wine
and evening pilgrim meals with garlic soup
while resting weary, blistered feet
and sharing kindred pathway memories.

Walking now alone on dusty paths,
my thoughts relive a daughter's dreams
of sharing Spanish pilgrim trails
with father close and by her side.

Instead she walked long grimmer trails,
indeed with father by her side,
but now down long hospital halls
and hope denied at every turn.

Today, on ancient trail with staff in hand,
my footsteps pound out mantras of remembrances,
fondest memories of camino walk with son
and those more grim of daughter's hope-dashed dreams.

KAFUMBA

Weeds grew tall in the red laterite road
between massive mango trees laden with purple fruit
as we inched up the slight rise in lowest gear.
Kafumba, old mission station, haven of peace in former years.

We rounded a curve, and there at hilltop as sun dropped low
stood roofless walls, doors and window frames removed,
Beneath the word "Clinique," hand-lettered,
a rusty bicycle frame stood tirelessly against mossy bricks.

In what was once a garden, straggly red poppies lifted heads.
A wild dog, startled by our presence,
yipped and rushed into the banana grove,
disappearing in the gathering dusk.

Just six years before, imagine drums throbbing and songs arising
from the church now open to the season's rains.
Children's voices rang with happiness
from open schoolhouse windows.

Nurses in white uniforms
and women in brightly colored wax print cloth
walked with purpose, greeting those in need of doctor's care
or those eager to learn to decipher printed page.

But poverty and pain breed calls for change,
and revolution brings destruction,
roofs ripped off and doors and windows
then carted off for new construction.

What motivation lay behind those swinging machetes,
those flaming torches and sharpened axes?
Fear of losing long-time clan traditions?
Or simply have-nots versus those who had?

We watch the moon set behind Kafumba's broken walls
As ghosts of wide-eyed missionaries, all well-meaning,
share the evening mist with red-eyed rebel kin,
fellow citizens of this divided world.

OLD GRIST MILL WHEEL

The rusty water wheel still stands tall,
surrounded low by twisting vines
and high by willow branches,
some growing through the metal buckets.

In its prime, the wheel spun proudly
powered in the race by water rushing
down from high mountain springs
in its speedy course toward ocean.

Some wheels were built of chestnut,
solid wood and smooth to miller's touch,
spinning silently with the water's flow,
gathering deep green moss as years raced by.

This wheel, now silent, ribs of steel,
clanked noisily as on its axis turned,
and the awesome power it harnessed
made the driveshaft spin and miller smile.

The dusty miller, high on floor above,
poured burlap bags of yellow corn or winter wheat
down through the shoot to sturdy millstones
rumbling on the floor below.

The millstones, carefully dressed
by skilled stonecutter's hand,
were grooved to transform hard kernels
into meal for mush and flour for bread.

Each farmer carried home in fall
his sacks of meal and whole grain flour,
sweet sustenance of love for families
when pulled warm from stove or oven.

But radio waves then filled the night
with promises of super flours, light and white,
processed and bagged by modern city mills
and sold cheap in mammoth urban stores.

So now the rusty mill wheel idle stands.
With farms abandoned, the miller too is gone,
the millrace broken, the old mill itself in ruins,
and local whole grain flours a distant memory.

NATURE'S FIREWORKS

Why wait for pyrotechnic color
on Independence Day?
Through deepening dusk in early June
we slowly ventured up the twisting trail
in hopes of catching the Smokey Mountain's
firefly's synchronous display.

As darkness gathered on our narrow path,
and as a bend we rounded,
two dark shadows loomed up before us,
two elk, perhaps also waiting for the spectacle.
They slowly turned and disappeared
as silently as spirits through the trees.

An occasional ordinary firefly,
as in our lowlands, rose from mountain forest floor,
blinking intermittently,
and from time to time a rarer relative,
blue ghost, drifted low before our eyes,
its blue-green light a steady glow.

But we had come in great anticipation
to seek the legendary pageantry
of aerial dancers' synchronized performance
by *Photinus carolinus* in brilliant flickering delight,
a marvelously bright repetitive display
in mate-attracting sequence.

As we sat in darkest moonless night,
we shivered when on nearby slope
one lonesome elk raised bugle to his lips.

And further up the valley,
came the eerie answering call
of great horned owl on silent wings.

Then suddenly as if on cue,
by dozens, bright lights flickered in the woods,
each light blinking five, six times.
Then all grew dark, a time of rest,
some five full seconds or more,
and once again exploded in brilliant dots of light.

We watched in awe as angelic swarms,
first scores of these performers, synchronized,
then hundreds, impervious to our presence there,
displayed their natural intermittent brilliance,
five seconds on, five seconds off,
for others of their kind.

Why wait for pyrotechnic color
on Independence Day?
Just find a spot in hidden Smokey Mountain cove
in June on darkest, moonless night.
Then open wide your eyes
to the fireflies' synchronous display!

MOON OVER GAZA

Tonight, red tracers fill the darkened sky,
and the clatter of machine guns assails our ears.
On the shelf, dry crusts alone remain,
and the water jug is despairingly light
as we huddle under splintered roof.

We used to sit under waving palm trees,
sipping tea together in the jasmine-scented breeze.
Filtered through the rustling fronds,
soft peaceful light from waxing moon
would sparkle in your smiling eyes.

As the sun set over the western sea,
we'd watch each evening as moon grew full,
raising our spirits and lifting the tide of our hopes
that though refugees' status remained our lot,
a homeland might one day soon be ours.

Now too, though tank treads rumble and roar,
and laments of our neighbors fill the night;
though the stench of powder hangs on the wind,
a thin sliver of peace pierces the darkness
with the muezzin's pre-dawn call: "Allahu Akbar!"

So as we peer through cracks in concrete wall,
the slender crescent raises hope in western sky.
Though our fortune's tide now lies still at lowest ebb,
with Red Crescent help and support from friends,
a super moon will lift our sea of happiness.

DREAM PATHS

The path beaming from the half-moon
dropping in the western sky
filters through lace curtains,
and I rest on the edge of sleep,
faint images from hidden dreams
flickering ghost-like deep behind my eyes.

Vague memories of paths through village markets,
colorful, well-stocked stalls, with vendors' calls,
lie just out of reach of consciousness,
and I soar above thick tropical forests,
hearing from below faint echoes
of squeaking fruit bats and
the squawks of parrots.

Like blurry images from old slideshows,
narrow forest roads wind ahead,
rock-strewn mountain paths
lead on to unknown vistas,
and footsteps on the white sand beach
beckon me across the dunes
through the waving oat grass.

As sleep recedes,
the graying dawn awakens,
and the birds begin their chorus.
May I, inspired by shimmering dreams,
resolve to stride with purpose,
eyes open to note the beauty
of each small step on my path ahead.

FRUIT BATS

From my balcony tonight
I watch the moon hang heavy
over Lake Tanganyika.
In the distance,
from across the lake,
bursts of rebel gunfire clatter,
awakening my fears
and shattering the peace of villagers
huddled behind their mud-brick walls.

As I lament the ravages
of human enmities and strife,
the faint rustle of giant wings
and myriad clicks and squeaks
draw my vision upward.
Outlined against the moonlit sky,
the air is filled with undulating waves
of mammoth fruit bats,
thousands on their nightly flight
toward fruit-filled forests to the north.

In spite of bursts of violence
by human clans who vie for power,
nature's faithful rhythms carry on,
unswayed by human folly.
I watch as streams of darkened wings
pursue their ritual paths,
disregarding human hate and greed,
intent on nightly feasts of yellow-orange mangos,
tasty red bananas, and papayas golden ripe.

I sit through pre-dawn hours and wait
as moon drops low beyond the lake.
The gunmen tire, the night grows still.
As the eastern morning begins to gray,
a rustle returns with squeaks and clicks,
and the bats stream back
toward waiting daytime roosts
to hang in trees beside the lake,
affirming nature's faithfulness,
leaving tranquility in their wake.

HAIKUS INSPIRED BY RING LAKE

On distant mountain,
the ever-shrinking snow patch
reveals summer's green.

On the limber pine,
five needles in a packet,
forming community.

Moon's silver sliver
begins its rise toward fullness,
now cradling my dreams.

On the distant nest,
mother osprey feeds young chicks
and calls out her joy.

Tonight, in dark sky,
three stars form Triangle,
shaping summer nights.

Boulders lie jumbled,
mammoth heaps left by glacier,
what power in ice.

In the Badlands
the colors and shapes of rock
communicate beauty.

Summer's Ursa Major,
circling high above North Star,
ladles happiness.

REGRETS?

In any life, two roads diverge, or three.
In the distance, on the far-off horizon,
roadsides converge,
obscuring long-term hopes, goals,
and hidden dangers.
Which path to choose?
Would I regret the path ignored?
Would I one day say, "If only?"

Of course, consider pros and cons,
and allow your mind to sort and weigh.
But each new road may offer hints
of novelty, of adventure calling.
Looking back, how would the summer course
in Norway have changed my life?
An interest now perhaps in Nordic sagas
instead of Gallic courtly love.
Enhanced no doubt by teaching job
in Newfoundland and not in Africa
and language skill in old Norse
and not in mellow sounds and rhythms
of modern French.

The road not chosen
at each divergent point
would have surely led
to rich adventure,
to a satisfying life.
But the roads I chose,
by luck or intuition,
have opened gates of wonder
to a life with but one regret—
failure to offer deepest gratitude
for experiences rich and often unexpected
along my life's trajectory.

NIGHT SOUNDS

Over nearby hills the half-moon rises,
casting light through open blinds.
Croaking frogs toss full-throated calls
into the still night air.
Lifting head from pillow,
I marvel, resting in that nowhere space
twixt sleep and wakefulness,
at nature's nighttime sounds.

My mind turns back to other sounds
of nights near summer solstice
encamped by remote Alaskan glacier lake,
with just a hint of midnight darkness,
ear attuned to moose munching willows
and lonely calls of nearby loons.

The songs of frogs and loons
awaken memories of nighttime human sounds,
when kept awake in steamy darkness,
equatorial nights lit by Aladdin lamp alone,
by the rhythm of pounding drums
of dancing feet
and strummed artisanal guitars
at village celebrations.

I think as well of stormy, frigid night
in hidden mountain cabin, deep in woods,
with worrisome moaning wind
and ominous crashing sounds of falling trees
that dash the comforting lights
and bring impenetrable darkness,
keeping restful sleep at bay

Of that night in waring country
with screened windows opened wide
to welcome cooling early morning breeze,
jolted by a blast in near banana grove,
heart racing in panicked fear,
then calmed by ritual call from mosque
of muezzin inviting all to prayer.

My head returns to rest on pillow,
and as the moon continues to caress my face,
my arm confirms love's near presence.
Drifting back from wakefulness to sleep,
I offer thanks for cherished memories
of nighttime sounds in wondrous
corners of our home on earth.

WIND IN OUR VALLEY

From their homes on compass rose,
each wind brings voices to our valley.

West October winds sweep up the Swannanoa,
raising whitecaps on farmers' ponds,
sending red sourwood leaves into the air,
dispersing dandelion seeds and mushroom spores,
and carrying echoes of long-lost native accents
of men paddling round river's bends
to harvest from banks' fertile fields,
squashes, corn, and ritual tobacco.

Then boreal blasts cross craggy peaks,
outlined against December's cloudless azure skies,
lift soaring raptors, eagles, hawks.
We hear vague sounds of long-gone trappers,
seeking beaver pelts for felted hats.
Wind's winter frost shakes cedars, chills our bones,
but unveils as well night's starlit skies
and calls colors to our cheeks.

In gusty March, winds from the east
lift our hats, give wings to kites.
They bring their moist warm breath to sage
and other myriad floral lives.
We catch the distant echoes
of ancient hammer strokes on railroad spikes,
the moans of laborers forced to work,
and creaks of wagon wheels as settlers
with muffled Scottish brogue
swept through the mountain passes.

Late summer storms, the hurricanes,
are full of whispers from far-off southern shores,
accents Cajun, Spanish, Creole, French
from ocean waves, Antillean isles,
and Mississippi delta.
Their welcome rain ends summer's drought
and conjures up red cardinal blooms,
caressing sweetgrass for winter braiding.

From west, from north, from east and south,
our valley winds bear history, wisdom,
life, and welcome inspiration.

INSPIRATION ON THE BEACH

The artist vision scans lakeside beach,
seeking inspiration in color and shape.
Superior's storms have rolled the rocks,
smoothing corners and leaving rounded forms
in heaps on the white sand.
Cupped in hand, smooth surfaces
show their colors—red, blue, and green—
and impart serenity with their touch.
On this beach in distant times
Ojibwe braves would beach canoes,
as would *coureurs des bois*,
seeking sustenance in the fertile wetlands.
From 'neath the mounds of rounded stones,
today you pull a rough-hewn grayish shape,
a wondrous geode
formed so long ago in limestone.
Cracked open,
will it reveal its blue, its green,
its purple crystals
and trigger colorful forms
in the artist's mind?

"THE MORE THINGS CHANGE"

In French, there's a saying,
"the more things change,
the more they stay the same."

But just watch the valley rivers
in the hurricane's path
as they overflow their banks
and leave deep red scars
in the wooded slopes.

Or listen to the mournful wail
of mothers in Gaza towns
after the rat-a-tat-tat
of enemy fire
leaves bodies still on ground.

And think of visit to coastal woods
along Atlantic shores,
all senses shocked
that in a few short months
the ocean waves have pushed back
the wooded shore
by meters, not by feet.

And, too, we long for discourse
in our public spheres
that clings to truth and civil words.
But all has changed,
and now the waves are filled
with voices spouting hate
and reveling in lies.

So clearly all things change.
Will they not one day
change for the better?

DESERT MONSOON

It's late July, and springs
that gush from Organ Mountains
throughout the year
have weakened to a drip.
Hillsides rise brown against the pale blue sky.
Mule deer lie panting in the shade,
the dusty snakes can scarcely rattle,
and roadrunners slow to walk.

Then, as the scorching sun
begins to drop in west,
the sky turns black,
and we watch from mountain slopes
as rainstorm sweeps across
high desert valley, blotting out the sun,
led by gusty winds that bring
all plants aquiver
with great anticipation.

The cooling storm drums
like thunder on our red tile roof.
From downspout, gushes welcome rain
toward thirsty kitchen garden,
where cayenne peppers and tomatillos
await monsoon's restoration.

Then, after first monsoonal rains,
August's morning sun
peers over eastern mountain peaks
at newly blossoming barrel cactus,
floral gold and orange,

at Indian paintbrush, scarlet red,
tall bull thistles, magenta hued,
and lemon-yellow columbines,
exploding colors on brown desert rock.

Mule deer race to the gushing spring,
freshly washed rattlesnakes
shake their glistening tails,
the roadrunner begins his grateful dance,
and humanity awakens
to a new creation.

HUMMINGBIRD IN RAIN

Hummingbird sits on the thin branch
in the pouring rain,
throat dull ruby under leaden sky,
wings stretched from time to time,
shaking off the water.
Drops of water
glisten white on tail feathers
at the end of summer
in the chilling rain.

He dreams of tropic's rain
in warmer lands,
where his name will change
to Colibrí or Picaflores,
takes final sips from the pink phlox
blooming late with fading sweetness,
good energy for the journey.

He plans his route,
myriad non-stop miles
across the Gulf, wings beating
perhaps one hundred times each second
with his mate,
both longing for tiny hidden flowers,
white and nectar-rich,
nestled deep between
the bougainvillea's magenta bracts.
And for bird of paradise, brilliant orange,
plus a multiplicity of orchids,
yellow, purple, or blue,
snuggling in the arms of trees.

Following nature's laws
in April next with mate,
he'll swoop and dive,
ruby throat glistening in the light,
both delighted once again
to finish trip back north
and feed from newest blossoms
in Carolina spring.

COME WALK WITH ME

Come walk with me
and sense the earth
beneath our feet.

Feel the soft and shifting sand,
when rising over crest of dunes
we stand in awe of ocean's broad expanse.

Imagine walking through cloister gardens,
missal open, deep in prayer,
enhancing mindful meditation.

Or like a pilgrim striding on camino trail,
staff in hand, being first to see
Santiago's cathedral towers.

Then we may stroll in city park,
hand in hand by river's edge,
past graceful floating swans.

Welcome breezes ruffle hair
and sunshine, warm, caresses cheeks
as muscles flex in rhythmic motion.

We keep both eyes and ears alert,
pace unhurried, enfolded in the arms of nature,
all worries left behind.

And now can spot the tiny flowers
of crane fly orchid on mountain trail
or hear the wood thrush sweetly sing.

We place one foot before the other,
allowing each to lead in turn
and all heavy cares to drop away.

CULTIVATE YOUR GARDEN

"Cultivate your garden,"
says Voltaire's Candide
after wandering the earth
and seeking hopelessly
the best of all possible worlds.

As I survey my garden,
pulling small maple sprouts and crabgrass
from the mulch under my blueberries,
I reflect on cultivation,
on improving, on encouraging growth,
on nourishing the positives.

May I cultivate my vision to notice
each small beauty from the tiniest flower
and the swelling buds on berry bush
to the every-changing shapes of clouds
in the blue Carolina sky.

May I cultivate an attitude of joy,
brightening my garden,
my little corner of the world,
pulling out the weeds,
not only tiny maples, ragweed, dock,
but also weeds of self-pity, of disappointment,
and of unworthiness
so that healthy growth may flourish.

CELEBRATION IN TIMES OF CONFLICT

Staccato machine-gun fire
echoes in the hills above:
daily occurrence in this civil war

marching boots pound by
in the street outside
past the locked wooden gate

under tent in courtyard
sits bride enthroned, dressed in white
with flowered turban

maternal uncle, first in French,
then Kirundi, announces impressive
bride price, expressed in cows.

waiters carry oblong silver platters
laden with rice and multicolored beans,
chunks of Muramvya cheese

golden slices of papayas, mangoes,
and honey-sweetened cups
of shade-grown mountain coffee

acrobatic drummers share their skill
honoring bride and groom
in rhythm with their kindred hearts

and drown into forgetfulness
the threatening sounds outside the walls
of hillside guns and pounding boots.

SOURWOOD SOLILOQUY

I'm always first in autumn season
to transform my greenery
to brilliant red.

My trunk, with rough-hewn alligator bark,
in every season seeking sun,
twists through forest understory
as if shaped by sculptor's hand.

In August's warmth,
sweet nectar in my blossoms
invited swarms of honeybees
to make their sweetest honey.

And now, with October rains,
my crimson leaves have lost their color,
dropping to the ground
when autumn gusts pierce mountain pass.

Winter days draw nigh,
and I will then stand leafless, bare,
but sentinel to permanence
of nature's constant cycles.

For in few short months will swell
new buds and tender leaves appear,
announcing verdant glow, then crimson joy,
and summer scents and sweetness.

HERON TEARS

Dew droplets sparkle on tips of grass.
Moist morning fog caresses us softly.
Watercolor brushes touch cheery color
to waiting paper,
blue and yellow creating green,
the vibrant color of life.
Thirsty plants bow in gratitude
for welcome drops;
canteens yield precious liquid
on summer mountain hikes.
Baptism in peaceful river cleanses soul.
Water, the faithful source of happiness.

But its beauty turns destructive
when over warming seas
the whirling winds give weight to clouds
and send them rushing north,
bearing treachery and pain.

The rising tide sweeps over
barrier strands, churning streams of sand.
Each wave surges, digs deep channels
through the island roads.
Relentlessly in flooded rivers,
mud-red dye slips
through cracks in doors
and over thresholds,
soaking ancient Persian rugs
in sad, dull watercolor hues.

Torrential rains in mountains
fill valley streams with raging foam,
sweeping trunks of trees,
tossing cars like toys,
ripping homes from their foundations,
destroying life and dreams.

And then the moisture-laden clouds move on,
leaving in their path
long deep red gashes
on green Carolina mountain slopes,
splintered mud-streaked buildings,
broken roads, and shattered lives.

And as belated sun appears,
blue heron beats his doleful wings,
drops sadly
to the battered riverbank,
surveys the scars and rubble,
and with grieving families
weeps his heron tears.

BEAVER IN STORM

My broad flat tail
slapped joyously on water's surface.
Steadily, some welcome rain had fallen
and creek replenished.
I heard the sound
of splashing water,
and whenever rushing water
echoes in this valley,
with joy I seek to show
my engineering skills
and build my dam.

My friends and I
pulled sticks, tooth-sharpened,
from bank beneath our lodge
and placed them carefully,
packing dam with creek-bed clay
in all the cracks.
We swam contentedly
in our deepening spring water pool.

Then tornadic wind began to stir,
and steady rain increased
and turned to downpour.
Creek water rose
as torrents gushed
down mountain slopes,
laying bare deep red gashes
and breaching banks.
Through the long night
we clung to saplings

bent low along the riverbank
as dam with logs and even rocks
careened downstream,
carried off by raging waters.

When daylight came and clouds dispersed,
our tearful eyes
beheld the desolation.
Our lodge was washed away,
and all the sweet bark sapling logs
set aside for winter meals had disappeared as well.

We looked each other in the eye.
I dove into the turbid water
and slapped my tail to vent my anguish.
Then climbing high
above the ravaged riverbank,
I sank my teeth in maple wood
and began my chosen work again.

LAND MINE

In that mountain city,
many streets unpaved,
just hard packed dirt.

Armed conflict, civil war
raged in nearby mountains,
gunshots echoing day and night.

Then came the warning:
"There may be landmines
buried under unpaved streets!"

Venturing out to market,
I would lightly tread, eyes down,
thinking that if I lost a leg

I would take my crutches
and hop one-legged

to sit in protest
at the landmine factory's gate.

GRENADE AT NIGHT

Heavy curtains drawn,
as security expert advised,
to protect from shards
of shattered glass

All afternoon the heavy boots,
not of soldiers but of politicians'
unofficial private gangs,
have rattled windows

Windows closed, lying in sweat,
fearing that the guns and bombs
of civil war this night
might tear apart the sleeping city

As half-moon slowly rises over mango tree,
casting its partial light on city streets,
a grenade explodes by garden wall,
shattering the night and splintering windowpanes

Then, proposing a competing claim,
the pre-dawn muezzin's call from mosque
rings out with sounds of peace,
calming deep-set fears and reigniting hope.

HIDDEN LIFE IN BLEAK MIDWINTER

Dark maple limbs stand upright,
stark against the steel gray sky.
Mist inches down the mountain slope
shrouding human spirits.

A time of introspection.
Our thoughts turn inward,
conserving strength and making
plans for days ahead.

All leaves have fallen,
and tree canopies
stretch barren branches
toward low-hanging clouds.

But in bleak midwinter,
as humans build reserves
and plan for days to come,
nature's hidden forces thrive.

The trees' fine root hairs
reach out toward water,
soak up nutrients,
and connect with fungal threads.

Though days are short,
Our fingers touch at end of twigs,
unexpected leaf buds swelling,
harbingers of spring.

Midwinter then is more than bleak
as hidden forces move and swell,
a guarantee that someday soon
the earth will green again.

MULLING

The fierce north wind sweeps down
between the treeless mountain peaks,
its chill inviting all to shelter,
mulling over past year's memories.

We dream of springtime sun
that warms the waiting soil
and coaxes dormant seeds
to push up their tender leaves.

We think of hiking mountain trails
through green rhododendron tunnels
and under blossoming sourwood trees
in August's sweltering heat.

But now, in deepest wintertime,
flakes of snow swirl thickly past our windows,
and barred owl's plaintive call is muffled
by the wind chime's clamors in the night.

Star anise, cinnamon from exotic lands,
peel of orange, zest of lemon
surprise the air with fragrance,
the welcome scents of spicy wine.

Long gone the heat of summer days,
but with the glow of candlelight
and these seasonal olfactory delights,
our wine well-mulled cheers heart and soul.

RUB A DUB

I gather my rosemary and thyme,
some onion and garlic powder,
and a little pepper and salt
for my Thanksgiving turkey rub.

And as I consider that rub
and the tub of peeled potatoes,
I think of those three men
who found themselves in a tub.

The butcher had brought to market
and sold his thick T-bone steaks.
The baker brought his dozen
tasty hot-cross buns, all thirteen.

The candlestick maker waxed eloquently
about his nicely turned oak holders.
They were all three upright citizens,
wealthy, fat, and respected in the town.

But why did they discard
breeches, cloaks, and aprons?
Maybe on a dare
from the Merchants Guild.

The young town lassies giggled
and jeered as they walked by.
And I chuckle too at the thought—
three chubby bodies so like my fat turkey.

EDELWEISS

Your petals, in true discretion,
lie quietly in the alpine meadow.
Not like tall-stalked hibiscus flashy red
or like sky-blue asters growing wild
or strapping sunflowers gold and yellow.
Your small white blossoms,
shaped like a lion's foot, barely rise
above the pale gray leaves,
spreading flat between lichened rocks
at highest elevations.

But to the traveler, staff in hand,
who seeks to cross high mountain passes
and breathes the pure thin air
under pale blue summer sky,
your presence, covered months by snow
and buffeted by hail and wind,
faces skyward toward the sun
in June and shows the traveler
that a hardy tender soul
with fortitude and courage
can weather storm and pain
and yet display its beauty.

EROSION

The rushing water
scours riverbanks of the mind,
uproots trees and buildings,
and gouges canyons in the red clay,
exposing rocks
digging deep into the psyche,
ripping away protective forgetfulness
and exposing memories,
raw and painful,
of hurtful words expressed in anger,
of hidden shame
glossed over by bluster,
of deeds undone,
smothered in laziness.

Down at bedrock,
washed clean of silt and guilt,
human kindness is now laid bare,
and resilience can reappear.

MUTUALITY

On a busy city square
of the town in southern France,
a bronze statue draws my eye.
A blind man strides ahead,
unseeing, of course,
but confident in his path,
on his back a crippled guide
who hasn't walked for years,
but who can reach his destination
when carried by strong legs.

And below I see gray lichens,
festooned on statue's base.
Some lowly formless algae, to build
a lichen that can thrive on hostile ground,
have linked with partner fungi
to give a form, protection.
In recompense for shape and strength
the algae provide its partner food,
with chlorophyl create the sugars
that power the lichen's growth.

Without his crippled guide,
the blind man could never find his path.
Without his strong and sightless friend,
the lame man only creeps and crawls.
Without the fungal strength,
the algae have no shape.
Without the algae's energy,
the lichen cannot grow.
When equal partners
share their symbiotic gifts,
greater is the whole
than of the parts the sum.

WALKING, WALKING

As a child, skipping barefoot in the grass,
seeking fireflies in the gathering dusk,
I save their yellow glow in Mason jar
to light my onward path.

Or then, feet pick their way through branches,
limbs, and rocks left bare by hurricane,
and I marvel at the fearsome power
of rushing water.

Perhaps, at other times, like Johnny
with pouch of apple seeds,
seeking fertile loam,
I spread new plantings as I walk.

John Muir, too, would leave on foot,
for days and often weeks
up rocky forest slopes,
exploring mountain wonders.

Like Rousseau, emulating Noble Savage,
I may wander pensively through orchard, glen,
and step by step through twisting mountain passes,
untainted by corrupt society.

At one with lichens, mosses, flowers,
and stately forest canopies,
I ambulate in nature as in my cloister,
an open field guide for my prayers.

THE HAPPINESS QUOTIENT

Economists and politicians
watch the GDP
and cheer its rise
or lament stagnation.
But do they care to watch
the mercury rise or fall
in the gauge
of Gross Domestic Happiness?

Do they measure
the subtle reddish hues of buds
on maple trees in spring?
What units do they use to mark
the cheery song of mother wren
that greets us with the rising sun?
Can they calculate
the clarity of winter sky
and awesome might
of those celestial wanderers:
Mars, Jupiter, Venus?
Do they sense when breeze blows cleaner
and our streams run clearer?
Where is the instrument that can gauge
the warmth of crooked smiles,
the joy of job well done,
the assurance that
our government is for the people,
all citizens, my neighbors?

May economists and politicians
keep one eye on the GDP
and with the other observe
and cheer the rise
or lament the fall
of the elusive Happiness scale.

BLUEBERRY GRATITUDE

By the handfuls, hands now stained blue,
I fill my pail with gratitude and berries.
The laden bushes yield their bounty
and think back with thanks
to all the help their partners shared:

–The rich dark sandy loam
  gave support, protection
–Lowly earthworms enriched
  that soil with oxygen and nutrients
–Warm sunshine and gentle rains
  caressed their leaves
  and bathed their roots.
–The weeks of freezing days
  brought the needed chill
  to set the buds that bore the fruit.
–I, who pruned away dead wood
  and opened bush to light.
–Lumbering bumblebees,
  who sought out the nectar
  of the small white flowers
  and spread their golden pollen.
–And even thieving catbird,
  who stole some early berries
  and gave the others space
  to swell and sweeten.

At home, I spread my treasure,
plump and juicy blue,
on tartlet dough,
thanking generous berry bushes
but remembering, too, with gratitude
the loam, the sun and rain,
the freezing winter hours,
the birds and bumblebees.

NUIT DE SAINT JEAN

Hefty piles of sticks and logs
lie waiting for the lighted match
to lift great flames
of St John's solstice fire,
to keep at bay unkind spirits
seeking space in human minds
as sun turns south.

Then, as we circle hand in hand
around the blazing fire,
flames fly high into the air
this St. John's Eve,
scorching unkind spirits' wings
and sending them shrieking
into midsummer's air,
leaving us at peace.

DISCOVERING RED SHIRT LAKE

Packs strapped on backs,
near midnight, we start first trip
down the trail in arctic dusk
three miles up hill and down
toward summer's work-site cabin,
bear bells ringing as we walk.

Trees hang dark against the pale sky,
sun hidden just below horizon.
At a curve in the trail
we stop in fright at the whoosh
of startled spruce grouse family
launching into the air.

No mother bears protecting cubs
on this trail in dusky light,
but at a creek a bull moose stands
in water, crunching willow,
and motionless we watch
until he ambles off into the brushy woods.

As we crest the final hill,
a broad lake glimmers in the evening dusk,
and a pair of residents,
trumpeter swans, pure white,
gracefully swimming by beaver lodge,
bids us warm welcome
to our summer home on Red Shirt Lake.

OSPREY AT RING LAKE

The sun begins to drop
behind towering western peaks.
Patches of summer's lingering snow
stand out against the alpine meadow.

Above the shimmering lake,
the osprey circles in to waiting nest,
three gaping beaks anticipating
the wriggling fish in talon's grasp.

She casts a baleful eye
on fleeting passing human forms,
equating them to ancient flint-hewn
petroglyphs on lakeside red-rock cliffs.

Through countless generations
as human figures hunted bighorn sheep
or glorious landscape photographs,
osprey have kept their faithful watch.

NATURE'S BOUNTY

Shiny red clusters
of high-bush cranberries
catch the eye,
and I dream of bitter fruit
that cooked and sweetened
makes tart but tasty jelly
to pair with Roquefort cheese.

In sunny open space
beyond hill's crest,
blueberries lie ripening
on the slope. I beat the bears
and fill a pail
to add to yoghurt breakfast bowl.

Not far beyond
the wondrous sight
of long tall canes
bending heavily, laden
with fat red raspberries,
the regal fruit for tartlets
best served with fresh gelato.

It's August,
and on Alaskan trail
to ranger station
the canes and stalks and bushes
extend their hands to me
with gifts of taste and color.

FRIENDLY FLAMES

Though fire can be destructive,
we thank that Titan long ago
who braved the gods
and brought a flame to humankind.

We gladly cherish fireplace glow
that with its flickering blues and reds
both warms the heart
and calms the mind.

We watch enthralled the dance
of mesmerizing campfire flames
that call forth shivering ghostly tales
craved by eager wide-eyed campers,

Or the warming glow of candlelight
at tips of stately tapers
that grace a table shared
and light the tasty wonders.

Even fires in forests
can sometimes bring new life,
for seeds of longleaf pine
need trial by fire to germinate.

And villagers in Africa would burn
their fields before the planting
to rid the land of residue
and counter weeds and pests.

So fire, the welcome stolen gift
Prometheus brought to earth,
though truly fierce and dangerous
enhances all our lives.

BEGINNING

By the banks of the Kwilu River,
nestled among palms and papayas,
the little mission hospital, whitewashed
after deepest dusk, reflected light
from moon rising full and golden
through leafy branches of mango trees.

The first-born child had just voiced
his greeting to the earth at night,
cry echoing through the silent halls,
blending with the snorts and grunts
of hippos lazing in dark river's current
and the buzzing of ravenous mosquitos.

Now out on truck bed he lay in mother's arms,
wrapped in purple wax-print cloth
that in the pale moonlight
glowed in harmony with blossoms
festooned above in moonlit jacaranda trees,
his open eyes drinking in first beauty.

Fruit bats flitted across the moon
now risen, losing golden hue,
circling over treetops,
and staring down as young child
relished first nocturnal scents and sounds
of unexplored new world.

The truck rolled slowly over rutted ground,
its movement a simple foretaste
of grown man's delight in later years
in exploration of varied lands,
the wind speaking softly in the trees
foretelling adventures multilingual.

NIGHT THOUGHTS

Below the continental shelf,
deep in murk and gloom
awaiting filtered, shrouded sunlight,
nascent life moves slowly,
spinning thoughts before the cusp of dawn
in somber shadows of ancient griefs
and darker hues of tasks undone.

Crashing, silt-filled breakers
smash against the edges
of sleep and wakefulness,
currents dragging particles of mind
and bits of evolutionary growth,
the clicks and clacks of sound
and formless images from years gone by.

Will these primitive thoughts
one day slither out of murky liquid home
and stand upright on solid sunlit ground?

RED-TAILED HAWK

May my vision stay sharp
like the red-tailed hawk's.
He sits high on the tall white oak
or soars above the mountain top,
picking up the slightest movement
in the world spread below.

May I watch for colors, textures,
and unexpected movement, shapes,
on mountain slopes or forest floor
and be alert both to lines of care
and to the wrinkled smile
on the face of the beloved.

HOBO, EIGHT YEARS OLD

He had just turned eight years old.
He finished *Treasure Island*
and was dreaming of adventure.
He slipped on his favorite hat,
found a long straight stick
back where the hedgehog lived
hidden away and appearing
only in the evening.
Dug out his biggest bandana,
wrapped up his compass
and four KitKat candy bars,
then carefully tied the bandana
around the end of his stick.

He inched out the back door
and around the house
into the street,
stick over shoulder
and little canteen hooked
over his belt,
because he would surely need water.
Should he turn left or right?
He knew the ocean
was beyond the sunset,
and to find a ship
meant he should head west.

At the street corner
he stopped and ate a KitKat,
then a second
and took a sip of water.

Couldn't yet smell a sea breeze
or hear breakers crashing,
so he kept walking.
Reaching the park,
he sat down on the bench
under the plane tree.
Ate another KitKat
and then the fourth one.
Finished the water.

Still couldn't hear the breakers,
so set out again down the street.
Walked past the house
where Jean Ives lived,
but he wasn't outside.
Felt the bandana
at the stick's end.
Nothing but a little compass
bouncing around as he walked.
A little hungry,
but no more KitKats.

Perhaps he could explore the world
some other day, maybe the next.
He walked back down the street,
headed away from the breakers.
Opened the creaking gate
and slipped around the house
and through the backdoor.

HERON FISHERMEN

I remember, at the break of day,
watching great blue heron circle in,
with graceful wingbeats' slow descent,
to take their places round the pond.

Five tall curved-neck fishermen,
spread out around the water's edge,
each proudly occupying
his proprietary breakfast spot.

Like men in waders along Cape Lookout's shores,
waiting for the autumn run of blues
with lengthy poles and fancy reels,
they stood with sharpened beaks and watchful eye.

As I observed in morning light,
one sharp beak at lightning speed
snapped down to gather unsuspecting fish or frog,
and great blue faced his friends with heron grin.

Then others triggered breakfast catch as well
and danced about with satiated joy.
Soon all five fishermen unfurled their wings
and skimmed across the pond toward heron home.

NATURE'S LESSON

I lay on my back
in the patch of clover,
watching the diaphanous clouds
floating peacefully beneath azure sky.
My ears were open
to the distant domestic call
of red-tailed hawk to mate
and to the buzzing honeybees
as they sipped nectar
from the white blossoms
and dusted legs with pollen.

On that marvelous May morning,
the mountain slopes
were alive with harmony
of various shades of springtime green,
the poplar tulip blossoms glowing
red and gold in the noontime sun,
while the red-bellied woodpecker
joyously tapped out his rhythmic code
on the bare-limbed sycamore.

A world of harmony and joy,
devoid of tooth and claw.
I lay oblivious to pain or conflict.
All seemed at peace.
And then my eyes grew wide
as the red-tailed hawk swept
barely twenty feet above my head,
a struggling black snake
desperately twisting, writhing
in the hawk's clenched talons.

PARISIAN COBBLESTONES

On these modern narrow Paris streets,
I still see cobblestones from medieval quarry,
rounded, worn down by myriad footsteps,
with memories of children running barefoot,
of lantern-swinging night patrols
calling out their "All is well!",
of battle-worn knights in battle-scarred armor
mounted on tired but prancing steeds,
waving banners with the fleur-de-lys
as they carried welcome news to waiting king.

Those smooth round stones also remember
the lumbering oxen drawing rumbling carts
loaded down from fertile farms beyond the river
with purple turnips, carrots orange, and leafy greens
and even rarest prizes from newfound world,
golden ears of maize and juicy red tomatoes.
The clattering carts called out to cooks,
who rushed with wicker baskets
and pounding wooden shoes to be the first
to gather in for waiting master's table
the stuff of culinary delights.

Turning inward, those old stone pavers,
some ringed with deep green moss, still weep
at memory of revolutionary horse-drawn tumbrels
with noblemen seated despairingly on their benches,
eyes fixed on glinting blade suspended high
that soon would drop and shorten their existence,
while jeering ordinary men and women, too,
watched with glee and shouted hate,

not knowing that in just a few short months,
they could also face the same grim fate.

And now in '68, as armored tanks
rolled in to quell the rising tide that sought
new freedoms in eastern European lands,
Parisian students found that rounded cobblestones,
when pried with crowbars from the narrow streets,
became projectiles fitting neatly in their hands
to claim with force demands for change.
But then, after show of strength by order's forces,
those hands that once held stones
now hid the eyes that couldn't bear to watch
from garret windows as city paving crews
covered up the handy weapons and
shrouded centuries of memories and history
by layering asphalt to hide those cobblestones.

MELANCHOLY MOON

The moon, risen full and bright,
looked down on the orb
that spun beneath it,
first at skeletal concrete walls
that once stood strong
among the Gaza palms,
next at battle-scarred ravages
in the Ukraine hills
that once glowed golden
with fertile flowered fields,
then at the chaos unleashed
by our country's so-called
for-the-people government.

And the melancholic moon,
sad and weary of human greed
and proclivity toward violence,
high at midnight zenith,
hanging in earth's shadow,
began to slowly pull a veil across
its wrinkled, saddened face,
tears filling the craters.
The thin red veil wormed its way
across the dimpled surface,
turning tears and craters crimson.

No longer able to stare down
at human strife and conflict,
the Blood Worm Moon hung
hidden behind its shadowy shroud.
For early humans in this land

the moon drew up that veil
and changed its face to red
whenever love and kindness died.
And I watched this night in anguish,
wondering if the moon
could ever dry its tears,
cast off its shadows
and look down lovingly once more
at human brother/sisterhood.

PYRAMIDAL BEAUTY

Let imaginary gaze and curious thoughts
sweep over golden desert sands
and settle on great pyramids,
concentrating cosmic forces and
rising toward the sky above the dunes.
Imagine all three faces, triangular in shape
and splashed with vibrant color,
crimson red like old-time hollyhocks,
sunny hues of mountain goldenrod,
and azure blue like Carolina sky.

With nimble fingers you remake
the beauty of those ancient shapes,
creasing, folding, linking,
each facet of the tripartite form
enclosed by melded lines
of outward joy and inner peace,
of quiet resolve to share
the beauty of this world
with color, texture, structure.

Now our years have totaled five,
each year steeped in eagerness,
with acrylic paints or watercolor,
to create and recreate reflections
of this world, not just this year
of somber hues from stormy devastation
but once again with pleasing shapes
and photographic color that bring
our world and both of us
together with cosmic pyramidal power.

LUCKY THIRTEEN

Who says that the number thirteen
always brings bad luck?
On that lucky thirteenth of August
you first breathed the fresh Wyoming air
and took first looks at mountain slopes.

Perhaps a black cat crossed your path
in that first tender week,
catching your attention,
bringing deep appreciation
of living nature, birds, elk, and bears.

And then you may have said,
"Mirror, mirror, on my bedroom wall,"
and then bumped the little mirror
that shattered into shards of glass,
feeling inadequate to reflect
the beauty of your heart.

And as you crawled under leaning ladder,
you looked at wall and rungs.
The lines and angles imprinted
on your mind for future skill
of putting shapes on paper, canvas.

And as a toddler, opening small umbrella
inside your house must have surely
set the stage, not for creating rainy days
but for turning rain and pain
to rays of warmth and love.

So remember that thirteen
is not the harbinger of bad luck
but like lagniappes
and baker's dozens
has added extras to your life.

NEW CASTLE

Still today they call me Châteauneuf.
But now I am no longer new,
long centuries have passed.
Mossy stones have fallen
from my ancient castle walls,
loosened by years of probing roots
of poppies red and royal purple iris,
seeds planted by doves and blackbirds
perched to coo or sing melodious notes.

My gates were strong,
the moat was deep and clear,
the heavy chain on windlass
could raise or lower drawbridge
to keep at bay marauders
or welcome neighbor castellans.
And from my turret windows
high on this Burgundian hill,
the guards could watch
for glint of sun on metal
in the verdant valleys
below this hilltop home.

Now tiles lie broken on my roof,
and spiral stairways
have seen stone steps
worn down by centuries
of nobles strolling 'neath the tapestries,
servants carrying up the fireplace logs,
and men-at-arms clanking down
to reach the postern door.

Today my tourist gate has opened.
I have surely seen my better days,
and the weight of centuries
makes my shoulders sag.
But on this morn
when bright-eyed child with flaxen hair
in bright red dancing shoes
comes bounding up the well-worn stairs
with dreams of princesses
and valiant knights
cascading through her curious mind,
my heart leaps up,
my turrets smile
and heavy years grow light.

WHITE GOLD?

Shaking crystals into soups
or dusting crispy fries from France,
I think about the simple gift
of salt on dinner tables.

Some salters evaporate the salty sea,
in Brittany's Guérande
or in the South's Aigues-Mortes,
working under sun and ocean breeze
to bring white gold to hearth and kitchen.
Others in the Franche-Comté have learned
to pump the brine from deep below
and fill wide metal trays
they heat with charcoal from surrounding hills.
As white salt crystals take their shape,
those salters rake them out, biceps aching,
back in pain, standing sweaty
in the humid, salty heat.

From heated vats or evaporation ponds,
they build the piles of white/gray salt,
then fill burlap bags to be carried off,
worth more than gold or precious gems
to castles near and far in early days,
where humble servants salted meat,
preserved for lords' and ladies' tables.

In medieval France the salt was taxed
so royalty could fund its wars.
No hardship for the noblemen,
but tax hurt all poor folk who needed salt

to save their meager cabbage crop
for sustenance through winter's frigid days.
No wonder that the peasants rose
in revolutionary days,
demanding end to saline tax.

Now salt is cheap, no tax today.
Whether *fleur de sel* that's sourced from sea
or crystals formed from deep-well brine,
it adds its flavor to my soups
and helps my bread to rise.

IN GOTHIC CHAPEL

I sit alone in sacred space.
The light is dim, and silence overwhelms.
Outside, light drizzle taps against the glass.
Reports of violence and hate
echo clumsily through my restless mind.
Truth is now obscured by politicians' lies,
and leaders seek unfettered power.

Then high above in vaulted space,
the organ pipes begin to sing.
As their graceful notes soar up
in shapes like gothic arches,
the outside clouds disperse
and timid beams of light slip through
windows red and green and royal blue,
bringing peace to restlessness.

ALSATIAN SPRING

The snow has gone from off the peaks,
the ice on ponds has disappeared.
No need to heat ceramic stove
that warmed our home through winter's cold.

Pale green tendrils rise from ancient vines,
and from their winter home in Spain
first storks alight on chimney tops,
the surest sign of coming spring.

MY VINEYARD, MY HERITAGE

My hillside smiles toward the morning sun,
the vineyard's rows now green with springtime tendrils,
the broken stones between each row absorb sun's warmth
and release it slowly throughout the cooler night.

Centuries have passed since my family
first planted this Pinot Noir on stony slopes
and with utmost care encouraged fermentation
and preserved those grapes as deep red nectar.

Some vines produced for scores of years,
each new generation planting new, replacing old.
Some ancient vines have weathered three score years,
the wine from those old vines my pride and joy.

That liquid life sustaining generations,
the wine that ages now in oaken barrels,
reflects my mounting years, my heritage
of planting, pruning my Alsatian vines.

THE JOY OF SIDEWALK CAFÉS

Oh, the joy of stopping at cafés
on crowded Paris streets
and finding space in sidewalk shade
beneath the chestnut trees.
The waiter quickly takes our wish,
then carries out his tray
with tiny cups of coffee,
dark and richly aromatic,
each with sugar lump and gourmet treat.

With back to wall,
we sit with eyes toward sidewalk,
watching people pass—
the housewife hurrying by,
her market basket filled
with yellow squash
and shiny purple aubergines,
and then a man with shiny briefcase
surely on his way to meeting
at the finance ministry next door.

We might well sit for hours.
Never would the waiter
ask us to relinquish seats,
our tiny cups of coffee,
rental paid, allowing us
to sit and marvel
at a moving universal stream
of multi-hued humanity
and offer thanks
for café's sidewalk charms.

GOLDEN MAGIC

Through fissures in the limestone
off the Jura's high plateau,
mighty rivers gush out from cliffs
to water valleys broad and green.
Those vibrant pastures, flower-filled,
feed a special race of cows whose milk
like magic turns to Comté cheese.

And surely magic it must be
when master craftsman heats fresh milk,
adds with care the dose of rennet,
and proudly watches liquid richness
turn to weighty golden wheels of cheese.
When aged and cut in perfect wedges,
that tasty cheese might well adorn my table,
a fitting end to gourmet meal.

PICK-UP-STICKS

Today a fierce wind whistles
in the estuary, raising foamy waves
and tossing massive logs
like tiny pick-up-sticks
against the palm-lined shore.
We dare not adventure to the beach.

In the forest tropical, those giant trees
once stood—the prized okoumé
and ebony and dark mahogany.
They cast their shade on birds of paradise,
their petals blue and orange,
and on the flame trees' vibrant scarlet blooms.

Then flocks of squawking parrots fled
as peaceful jungle silence
was rent by chainsaw roar,
long blades ripping through the bark,
the living cambium and the stalwart hearts
of these age-old forest guardians.

The giant timber lengths were dragged
to the river Ogooué and floated down
toward ocean port, where ships
would carry off those local forest treasures
to foreign lands and fatten foreign purses,
leaving naked hillsides to diluvian rains.

Some massive logs escaped that fate,
sometimes resting peacefully on the sandy shore.
We could often swim and drape
on trunks our brightly colored towels.
But not today! We can only watch
as wind and angry rolling waves
toss giant matchsticks to and fro.

ODE TO WATER POWER

(Inspired by the Taillanderie in Nans-sous-Sainte-Anne, France)

Oh, the marvels of the power of water
and of humankind's inventiveness!
In this metal-working shop,
where well before the age of steam,
workmen fashioned tools for home and farm.

Already centuries ago,
the brook's clear water
coursed swiftly through the race.
As wooden buckets filled,
the massive wheel would creak and turn.

Pure human ingenuity
linked the turning water wheel
to gears and belts that activated bellows
to furnish forge's oxygen
to warm and soften metal.

Man's genius over water
attached as well that driving force
to massive automatic hammer,
whose power when linked with workman's skill
turned formless steel to scythe and hoe.

Oh, water-driven workshop, symbol
of the beauty of the human mind
that transformed into energy and power
a swiftly flowing mountain stream,
creating tools for human use.

MARKET SEASONS

Each week I bring my produce
to the market in our village
to share with friends my cheery smile
and offer varied farm-fresh crops
my land provides for every season.

The winter has been long.
My wool scarf and stockings
kept me warm on market mornings
as I laid out displays of golden carrots,
cabbages, both green and white,
and parsnips, rutabagas, beets—
all you need for tasty winter grill.

The springtime comes with April showers
and sunshine warms the market square
as I unpack my garden's bounty:
tender snow peas, sugar snaps,
spicy radishes to crunch,
and lettuces, both red and green,
to serve with Dijon mustard vinaigrette.

I'm faithful, too, in summertime,
my garden's promises complete.
I offer you my crisp green beans,
which you enhance with almond slivers.
And baskets display my new potatoes,
peppers purple, red, and green,
and mounds of firm and colorful tomatoes.

When the autumn days grow shorter,
my scarf is welcome on cold mornings.
But faithful to my customers, my friends,
my stand is ready with the dawn.
My orange pumpkins will catch your eye
along with recipe for soup.
My broccoli is in great demand
as is the cauliflower you may prepare
with Comté cheese from neighbor vendor.

In every season my garden's wealth
will bring you flavor, color, health.
But best of all, we all enjoy
not only bounty from the land
but daily smiles of friendly neighbors.

PARIS STREET URCHIN

Twice he walked by pastry window,
lingering to survey the tempting rows,
tartlets—lemon, cherry, wild berry—
éclairs, cream-filled, with chocolate or coffee.

A ragged scarf hung 'round his skinny neck,
and mismatched shoes were worn and scuffed.
His woolen hat barely contained long strands of hair;
his eyes devoured the colorful display.

As I watched, a stately woman dressed in finery,
strode by with opera glass in hand.
Surely Verdi arias were coursing through her mind
as she hurried toward the nearby opera house.

But when she saw the ragged lad
staring hungrily through the glowing window,
she turned abruptly, and the door-chime
announced to waiting clerk her entrance.

Just moments later, back out she came,
one hand still held the opera glass, but in the other
lay a small white box with wide green ribbon
tied around in festive bow.

She motioned to the staring waif
and handed him the treasure box.
His eyes reflecting deep surprise,
he eagerly stretched out both grubby hands.

"Merci, madame," he did not fail to say,
then carefully, with great anticipation, undid the bow
and pulled away the paper to reveal
a waiting lemon tart and chocolate éclair.

The stately woman with her opera glass
hurried on to savor *Rigoletto*,
but leaving in her wake a grateful child,
touched this night by human kindness.

STORKS ARE BACK!

Today as I awoke,
I heard a clattering on the chimney top.
It's April, and the storks are back,
chattering in their Alsatian dialect,
their annual trip complete,
faithful purveyors of good luck!

I imagine that weeks before,
they left their winter home
in Spain, near Mérida,
where they enjoyed the sun
and culinary delights
of rodents, fish, and insects.

They crossed the dry meseta,
greening now in spring,
then raised high by updrafts
above the snow-capped Pyrenees
moved slowly up the Rhone Valley,
pausing frequently for sustenance.

So now again today
I watch them carry sticks
to fortify their mammoth nest
where soon the eggs will hatch,
and eager storklings clack
impatiently with open beaks
for bounty gathered from between
the greening vineyard rows.

As my family has for centuries
marveled at white storks' return,
announcing links with past tradition,
re-emergent spring, and hope renewed,
I too this day can praise the cycle
once again complete.

BREAD

"Long as a day without bread"
goes the French saying, unbearably long,
like sitting through a boring speech
or waiting for Christmas morning.

So any day with bread speeds up,
and all you need to do is open
bakery door, smell the rich aroma,
and marvel at the breads behind the counter.

But which to pick? I pick all three.
A golden-crusted baguette, well done,
a tangy sourdough *pain de campagne*,
and hearty full-grain *pain complet*.

My baguette delights at morning coffee
with strawberry jam or red currant jelly
and then at end of gourmet repast,
spread with goat cheese, brings ready smiles.

My buttered sourdough country bread
is perfect paired with radishes in spring,
and the full-grain *pain complet*
completes my French green lentil stew.

And if next morning, slices still remain,
all is not lost. Dip them in egg and milk,
sauté them crispy brown, enhance with jam or syrup.
All bread can still make days seem shorter.

MARAUDERS

I've grown used to visitors
to my blueberry patch.

Year after year,
the gray catbird sits in maple tree
and sings his litany of thanks
before swooping in and choosing
berry, just turning blue from pink,
and returning to his perch,
the berry in beak
hiding satisfied smile.

Robins, gregarious as they are,
arrive together chirpingly,
each choosing a separate bush
to rob of berry bounty.
And, too, brown thrasher couple,
pleased most days to scratch
mulched ground for insects,
flies up, sharp beaks glistening
in the morning sun,
to seek plant sustenance.

But today a special visitor
has found my berry patch.
An adolescent rabbit bobbed in,
stood tall on strong back legs,
white fluffy tail beneath,
and with his forearms
pulled down a laden branch,
lips closing 'round the ripening fruit.

I planted berry bushes
so that I could savor
at my morning table
the sweet blue antioxidants
and nets could guard the prize.
But that would dampen joy I feel
to share my berry bounty
with birds who sing their gratitude
and the adolescent rabbit
whose dances speak his thanks.

HUNGER IN GAZA

My little daughter whimpers,
bony fingers clutched to chest,
curled up on mat under refugee tent,
asking for water, bread, or anything
to dull her empty stomach's pain.

But helicopters throb above,
machine guns rattle
in Mideastern summer sun,
and neighbors, waiting at the square
for promised food relief,
scream and run for cover.

Meanwhile, in other nations,
there's willful ignorance of human pain,
and leaders seek to fatten their own purses
or use their power to protect their friends
and have no use for empathy.

My little radio brings bitter words
instead of hope, the news that at the border
many trucks, filled with flour and beans
and curative cans of fruits and meat,
are stranded, permission once again denied.

Next week, perhaps, the trucks might roll,
if machine guns cease their rattle,
and food might again provide new life.
But my own dear child before that day
will surely breathe her last.

HANDS

Under the mango trees
three children, their tiny hands
wrapped round juicy, red-skinned mangoes
that they had pelted down with rocks,
looked up and smiled,
lifting tiny juice-stained hands in greeting,
palms open and ebony fingers raised.

In the nearby market,
we strolled by nature's bounty displayed,
papayas golden in the sun,
mangoes, oranges, and limes,
then racks of salted fish
and stalks of sugar cane.

We marveled at mouth-watering scene,
delightful foods for every taste.
With images of juice-stained
waving palms still in our minds,
we passed the bush meat table
and gasped to see, their ebony fingers spread,
six tiny, severed monkey paws.

PILGRIM STREAM

Today my pilgrim path leads down
along a bubbling stream.
I've crossed the mountain pass
and pensively descend toward Santiago.

The water gushing from spring above
has bubbled forth for centuries
as pilgrims, tired but resolute,
passed daily, placing one sandal
in front of the other
as they had vowed to reach their goal
when leaving homes
long weeks before.

I, too, had vowed remembrance
of daughter who, before death took hold,
had longed to follow streams of life
and share my rocky path
toward distant pilgrim goals.

SUMMER NIGHT SOUNDS

The full moon rises over the trees,
dripping golden drops on quivering leaves
that rustle in the mountain breeze
and animate my dreams.

The old bullfrog, as he does most nights,
lifts up his raucous voice,
speaking words of love to partner,
nestled in mud at pond's grassy edge.

A barred owl, with soft wing flutter,
barely noticeable in the moonlit woods,
wraps talons round a branch
and calls out thanks for rodent prey.

In the distance, far over mountain peaks,
when pale blue lightning flashes
illuminate the darkening western sky,
thunder's rumble advertises summer storm.

As the Zodiac spins across the heavens,
I surely hear the fluttering pulse of light
completing journey from those far-off stars,
linking primal energy to all my dreams.

FIRST RAIN

Savanna grasses wave in the scorching wind,
brown and dusty, as dry season lingers
on the Congolese plains.
The river's current, usually strong,
carrying along dancing water hyacinths
and sometimes massive careening logs,
now flows serenely, exposing muddy banks,
the perfect resting place for crocodiles,
eyes nearly shut but watching, nonetheless.
Activity in the streets has disappeared.
Even drumbeats in the village have slowed.

On the rocks lie panting lizards, mouths ajar,
taking shelter in the shade of palm-nut palms,
whose fronds, though hanging motionless,
do harbor nests of gold-winged weaver birds,
too drained by season's sun
to ply their skill in fabric arts.
Even flies on kitchen walls remain lethargic,
unafraid of nearby geckos,
whose pale green translucent skin
can scarcely hide their skeleton.
Normally feasting voraciously on flying bugs,
they now themselves lie sleeping, waiting.

Then, in the tree outside my window,
the blue turaco squawks his clarion call,
announcing darkening sky in west.
The wind begins to rise, dust devils
swirling in the dusty path,
as market women gather up

their unsold red tomatoes and yellow mangos
and rush down that dusty path
to find their thatched-roof shelter.
Soon heavy raindrops pound on metal roof,
the geckos on my wall begin to stir,
and outside my window the blue turaco
opens wide his beak to gulp first welcome drops.

That longed-for drumming on my roof announces
joy at coming village celebrations,
where rhythmic drum and joyful dance
remind us all that in the coming weeks
the fields will all be hoed and hilled
and sprout their green with myriad shoots
of yams and corn and manioc,
after first welcome storm of rainy season
that guarantees abundant sustenance,
fulfilling nature's faithful cycles.

SUMMER'S END

As our hummingbird sips last sweet nectar
from hosta's final, purple-shaded blooms,
which, like magenta fireweed blossoms,
migrate relentlessly toward tall stem's end;

As the sun begins to inch back south
and our summer days, first by tiny seconds,
then by minutes, begin their slow collapse;

As the brilliant golden coreopsis flowers
begin to turn to dull-brown seed heads
that take unflattering name of tickseed;

As the blueberries, not long before,
glowing deep purple on leafy branches,
now grow sparse, stolen by hungry birds
and eager ink-stained human fingers;

As in late summer meteors make their annual visit,
flashing through the folds of Perseus,
shooting stars in August's nighttime skies;

May you remember that we live by cycles,
that the fireweed's disappearing color
announces maple's flaming red;

that these end-of-summer shortening days
portend the peace of longer nights
and fireside's warming glow;

that the brown-gray tickseed heads
will now be graced by feeding finches,
the male as golden as the summer flowers;

that sweet garden berries, the summer's bounty,
harvested by eager hands, now await
in freezer space for autumn's breakfast joy;

that nighttime skies will soon announce
the rise of winter constellations,
Orion and his dog, to grace the season's night.

May we not lament the fading marvels
of the summer's wealth and color.
And let us not despair, for summer's end
announces fall and winter beauty.

TROPICAL NIGHT

The night seems quiet,
but overhead the muted rush
of giant fruit bat wings,
tells us that the flock
is on its nightly quest
for ripened jungle fruit—
mangos, citrus, and bananas.
And the palm fronds
outside screened but open window
as they frame the Southern Cross,
rustle softly in the night wind.
In the distance,
the muted "hoo, hoo"
identifies an eagle owl
on its midnight predatory hunt.

Listen to the ripples
on the nearby darkened river
slapping quietly but insistently
against the colorful log canoes
partially beached at river's edge.
In the calm between the snorts
of hippos frolicking under starry sky,
we can even hear the broad leaves
of the bobbing water hyacinth
rubbing together as the current
pulls them irresistibly
towards the rapids waiting
noisily around the river's bend.

Then suddenly the night's serenity
is shattered by machine-gun rattle,
a grim reminder that human actions,
though sometimes warm and kind,
when based on greed or fear,
conspire to overwhelm
the peaceful sounds of nature's night
and turn our minds from calm to fright.

CAMINO WELCOME

I trudge along the dusty path,
twelve miles so far today
through waving fields of grain
on undulating meseta plains.
As I walk, the distant castle
grows its turret walls.

In medieval days that castle
was the stronghold of valiant knights,
the Hospitallers, who from their start
both guided and protected pilgrims
when Jerusalem was their goal.

As I approached those dark stone walls,
I could imagine knights, their armor
laid aside while watch they stood
on castle walls but ready
with their steeds if ever need arose
to sally forth to fend off highwaymen
from pilgrims, travel-weary like me today,
on their way to Santiago.

The castle gates swung wide
as I approached, my pilgrim staff in hand.
No armored knight did bid me halt
but wide-armed smiling guesthouse host,
and in the square a welcome feast was spread,
offering aged Manchego cheese,
newly chilled Verdejo wine
and tasty fresh-baked chunks
of full-grain country bread
from nearby fields of wheat.

TOWARD NOTHINGNESS

Along the winding mountain roadside,
the first pink blossoms of the fireweed
open wide to springtime's morning sun.
As the stalk grows thick and strong,
the welcome color migrates slowly upward.
Finally, as days grow short at summer's end,
the last blossom at tip of stem
fades and drops, announcing end of season.

On the flanks of these southern mountains,
in dark green stands, the healthy hemlocks
reached out and touched their neighbor's branches.
Then, as temperatures now grow warmer, no longer
can they thrive at altitudes they once enjoyed.
Each decade moves them higher on the mountain slopes
until, like the fireweed blossoms on their stems,
they drift off the highest summit and disappear.

A new world welcomes the child's first cry,
echoing through the hospital halls.
The voice then strengthens, learning harmony
and raising notes of joy and love.
Then, as months and years roll by,
the sounds that emanate begin
to wrinkle, folding back upon themselves,
until last rattle fades into the hospice night.

POWERLESS

Yesterday, three small goslings
walked single file, led by mother goose,
followed by attentive gander.
Today one is missing, quartet
swimming slowly, sadly,
wondering where that one has gone.

Could not the loving gander
protect and save his young
from roving hungry fox
or snapping turtle that lay await
beneath the murky waters of our pond?

Before, near Gaza's palm-lined coast,
parents watched in wonderment
as daughter, sprightly as gazelle,
would sing and dance to inner music
and leap into their arms.

What could the father do
when mortar rounds replaced the music
and food supplies all vanished,
leaving weakening, starving daughter
outstretched on death-bed mat?

And you, my daughter,
when you were small,
I soothed and comforted
after midnight frights,
provided love and beauty,
and lifted you from danger's path.

And now you, too, are missing,
snatched from fruitful joyous life,
leaving daughters of your own, of love bereft,
and grieving father who had not the power
to counteract the awful force
of human frame's collapse.

COLD AUGUST WIND

The wind blows cold in August.
My blood chills as bedside doctor
speaks today the dreaded words
"All we could do, we've done!"

And they had done so much:
transfusions, special medications,
hopeful words of comfort,
and hands of solidarity and warmth.

I remember clasping in my arms
the toddler, when you would wake in fright,
and later hand in hand I'd share the morning walks
toward school, and books, and friends.

And then, that day when dressed in white,
along the lakeshore, festooned in flowers,
you danced ahead, a strong adult,
needing no more a dad's protective arms.

But now today, the wedding dress
and boundless energy for life explored
have been replaced by pale white sheets
and swiftly fading dreams and hope.

The wind blows cold in August.
My blood chills as I watch in pain
and softly mouth the dreaded words
"May you rest in peace, my child."

BABY BELUGA LAMENT

What fun exploring river's depths,
where Arctic cod and octopus abound!
My dark-gray baby skin provides a camouflage,
but some day from gray I'll be a white adult.

My mother, as white as I am gray,
told me that in former years
the hunters, not called poachers then,
for oil would decimate belugas.

And still, she said, poachers remain,
and closest to my family pod,
I could be sure to find protection
and be guided clear of danger.

But then she said, as climate warms,
as the temperatures of our waters climb
and effluents flow from upstream factory pipes,
even greater dangers loom.

How can we navigate these poison seas
and find remaining ample stocks
of squid and fish and octopus
and clean glacial water to enjoy?

Alas, I fear that as the waters gray
and stench of chemicals pollutes my home,
I may never be a white adult
and live my years in pristine seas.

ANTICIPATION

The mother osprey circles high above the lake,
alert for underwater silhouettes.

The bearded miner, stomach growling,
sniffs the bubbling stew on tripod.

The blind man, his hearing super keen,
awaits first notes of Chopin's sweet études.

Drawing near the pastry shop, tastebuds quiver
at thoughts of cream inside the chocolate éclair.

The dry, parched throat and fevered brow
await a cooling sip and calming hand.

And shivers course through hand and mind
as silky skin responds to love's caress.

When drones and smoke trails streak across the sky,
we dream of shouts and cheers for peace.

RIVERS

Near rivers of my childhood days,
I learned that flowing waters cleansed the land
and brought rich life to thirsty plants.
They offered cooling pools for splashing boys
and seemed to wash away all earthly cares.

As darting dragonflies danced above,
in mountain streams the water,
singing words of peace and cheer,
babbled over rounded river rocks
where crawdads oft lay hidden.

On lazy summer days the fish
would rise to insects surface skating
on slow dark currents of coastal creeks,
and their rings of ripples showed me
where to cast my bait-filled hook.

And later, no longer as a child,
I made my home in equatorial lands
where rivers sprouted pods of hippos,
fish eagles whirled and dove for food,
and crocodiles could bask on sandy banks.

And then that fateful week in round Rwandan hills,
when once calmly flowing river changed its scope,
it carried rippled waves of vengeance, pain, and death,
mutilated bodies, chopped by knife, machete,
destroying peaceful images of rivers in my mind.

But now today, near Swannanoa's stream,
by singing willow shoots and wispy cardinal blooms,
as swooping swallows whirl in acrobatic spins,
nightmarish images depart, and peaceful dreams return.

BRISTLECONE PINE

You lie in pain, my daughter,
in the throes of dread disease
with unpronounceable name,
clinging to life as on a rocky cliff,
staring down at dark abyss below
and wondering how to cling to life.

Remember that tree on arid stony ground,
hanging firm above the void,
the ancient bristlecone pine
that has weathered endless storms
and kept a vibrant heart
against odds insurmountable.

PEACEFUL RIVERS

As black kites circled ominously above,
I ventured down toward the water
flowing through the country of the thousand hills.

I thought back to the rivers of my youth, so peaceful:
of mountain brooks bubbling over rounded rocks
that I could flip to find surprised gray crawdads
and where picnics lay spread in hemlock shade,

of lazy slower flowing flatland waters
with banks of pine straw's summer fragrance
where sunfish rose to surface water skaters
and showed me where to cast my line,

of rowing quietly on wider tidal creeks
soothed by the rhythmic splash of oars
and matching splash of jumping mullets
flashing white in the noonday sun.

I inched down slowly toward the river
that watered those green Rwandan valleys,
and slipping through the thorny thick acacias,
my stomach churned and legs grew weak.

For floating down the stream with reddish hue
were human torsos, arms, and legs,
machete-chopped by genocidal hate
and tossed like trash into the river
where marabout storks sat vulture-like in trees,
where hungry crocodiles thrashed and splashed.

I staggered back up through thick acacia thorns,
in anguish at the thought that human fears
could lead to such annihilation
and infect forever my images of peaceful rivers.

MORNING BLISS

Reluctant pigeons move aside
as eager waiter in white shirt
and shiny black bow tie
shows me to my waiting table
spread with plate of golden-brown croissants
and blue-white pot of red currant jelly,
sparkling in the morning sun
now rising from behind the Eiffel Tower.

The church bell chimes the early morning hour
and leaves of chestnut in the gentle breeze
drift slowly down to crunch beneath
the passing feet of neighbors rushing
toward the nearby metro stairs.

Behind the lace in upstairs window
across the busy street, old Madame Moreau
sits in her usual place, with tabby kitten
on her wheelchair's arm, watching life below,
remembering when she used to cross the street
to serve the morning coffee, jam, croissants.

As I sit, at nearby table the gentleman
with terrier on leash, who's there most days
but whose name I've never learned,
nods his polite bonjour and turns back
to brush off flaky croissant crumbs
from open book of verse by Baudelaire.

Then bow-tied waiter strides through open door,
on tray for me a steaming bowl of rich café au lait

and plate of tawny brown raw sugar cubes.
As the sweet aroma rises from the bowl,
I spread with care the currant jam on warm croissant,
lean back to lift a wave to smiling dame Moreau
and tabby cat enthralled by fluttering pigeons.
Then lifting bowl of fragrant coffee to my lips,
I savor welcome warmth of shared community.

MINING CLAIM

The golden eagle soaring in the sun looked down
on mountain meadow, the mass of golden banner flowers,
the purple sheen of squawking Stellar's Jay,
and scurrying cheek-filled chipmunks, pikas.

It was in late June, and except on highest peaks
the winter's snow had disappeared and flowed
in rushing rivulets down rocky slopes
to water verdant meadows far below.

Tin cup and shovel rattling on shaggy donkey's back,
the bearded miner finally reached his recent claim,
the narrow strip of land he would defend
in hopes of finding troves of gold or silver.

Through summer months he searched and dug
in lush green meadows, flower-strewn,
beneath wind-twisted stands of spruce
and under rocky cliffs with nesting peregrines.

At summer's end, just before first snow,
the eagle, soaring still above the flowery slopes,
watched the shaggy donkey and the shaggier man
start forlornly down, exhausted, sad, and empty handed.

RESILIENCE

Blue plastic tents stretched on forever
up and down the hillside,
row after row in endless ranks,
no trees for shade, no greenery to rest the eyes.

On his wobbly stool the old man sat,
protected by blue plastic from the sun,
clutching in his gnarled right hand
a battered pipe with no tobacco, only stains.

With massive crowds of other harried folk
he'd left his little plot of land, banana grove,
and limped for days to cross the border
seeking safety from genocidal threats.

He gestured toward me with his pipe
and told me with a crooked smile,
"Even here the human spirit
works, creating hope, community."

And I saw a woman in colorful wax-print cloth
braiding her neighbor's thick black hair,
their families crowding in great anticipation
around a bubbling pot of ground-nut stew.

I saw a teacher, with a make-shift slate
and clumps of charcoal that he used for chalk,
teaching eager children how to form their a's, their b's,
awakening curious minds to worlds of books.

Were I a refugee and had to flee my native land,
would I complain that life was gone forever?
Or might I, too, like these hardy souls in flimsy tents,
reach out to others and help affirm community?

SEED OF THE UNIVERSE

"In my breakfast bowl this morning,"
the old man smiled with teary eyes,
"unfolds the history of my ancestors.
I find once more the ancient sacred grain
that nourished family memories, this fonio,
no larger than a mustard seed, a seed
from which they say the universe was born
and which has found its way to my rebirth.

"On the dry West African savannas,
where New World crops like maize
have struggled in the desiccating winds,
this ancient grain can thumb its nose at drought
and once again has proved its worth,
nourishing the body, mind, and soul
as once it did for all the ancient ones.

"In my mind I see those mothers
from my family's distant past,
preparing for the rainy season,
bent but strong, and swinging heavy hoes
from blacksmith's magic forge,
casting seed that they had saved from years before
like memories of tales, of riddles, of speaking drums.

"This ancient seed from which the universe was formed
reminds me now today to relive age-old traditions.
I dream anew the secret songs, the wisdom,
the djembe's rich and rhythmic beats,
passed those many years ago in trust along to me
when as adolescent I conquered fear
and, braving ritual pain, became a man."

SOFTNESS

Life can be hard,
survival of the fittest,
some say,
and dog eat dog.

What brings softness
to your mind and heart?
Perhaps the kitten
curled in your lap,
the cheery song of the wren
seeking her spot for a nest;
Or the smell of ozone
with first drops of rain;
Orion the Hunter
rising in dark winter sky;
The baby's first cry
or grandfather's last breath,
those thin places
between worlds.

When life is hard,
and dogs are eating dogs,
may we stay open
to embracing softness.

GRAY FALL MORNING

Cool, gray fall morning,
and dancing in the east wind
are sourwood seed clusters
at the tips of branches
enfolded with scarlet leaves.

Who knew that the sourwood
was related to blueberries,
the blueberries whose leaves
are turning red in imitation
of their taller cousin
reaching high above them?

On the wrought iron
heron's back, a bluebird sits,
considering the protein rich
sourwood seeds. I watch
as it darts up to grab a seed,
or maybe an insect,
and return joyously
to his heron roost,
savoring it like a kid
licking a cone
in an ice cream shop.

DISAPPEARING MOUNTAINS

The mountains have disappeared,
hidden this morning by heavy fog.

Or perhaps while I sipped my coffee,
millions of years slipped by,
and the mountains eroded
to nothing, leaving flat plains
that turned to seabeds
as the oceans rose and
began to lay down layers of sediment.

And I wondered if in that time
the human race had completed
a slow return to its origins,
crawling back into the sea,
growing dorsal fins
or perhaps exoskeletons,
then finally becoming cyanobacteria.

I raise my coffee cup for a last swallow
and am surprised to see that
only minutes have passed
and that the dissipating fog
reveals these faithful mountains.

A NOVEMBER BLESSING

When darkness falls early,
the mind can fill with somber thoughts,
and the timid morning sun
is hesitant to rise;

When tree limbs stand
like dry bones
against the gray sky,
and all the leaves have fallen,
piled high like snowdrifts
against the garden fence;

When the last goose
has joined the V-formation
and headed south,
forsaking familiar pond
to escape the coming cold;

When the evening news
chills the heart
with shrill recriminations,
and reports of senseless wars
fuel the soul's deep anguish;

May you look for simple signs
of beauty, joy, and peace,
in lengthening night
as well as diminishing day:

The pair of mourning doves,
snuggling in sunshine on utility line,
a symbol of enduring love;

A thin crescent moon
in the Western evening sky,
promise of growth to fullness;

Orion the Hunter rising faithfully
in the late fall evening,
a reminder of nature's permanence;

The plaintive but sweet and loving call
of the barred owl to her mate,
echoing your beloved's caressing voice.

May your eyes and ears stay open wide
in daylight and in darkness,
to appreciate those tiny moments
whose power can calm all anxious thoughts.

WINTER FOREST BATHING

It's tempting on these winter days
to stay inside and dream of spring,
but don't forget your weekly forest bath
not far away on these mountain slopes:
a solitary walk through greenery and cleansing air.

Open wide your eyes to forest marvels
as golden sunlight filters through the twigs
enhanced by flash of blue as squawking jays
dart through rhododendron's twisting green
as leaves stay curled in the winter chill.

If you listen carefully, you can hear
the white oaks speaking lovingly to each other
as the wind caresses barren branches.
Their tender words and softer language
banish human shouts, recriminations.

Step onto the spreading beds of Galax,
their heart-shaped leaves now turning red
just in time to be true valentines.
Breathing in their pungency
can wash away all musty indoor smells.

Feel the crunch and crackle underfoot
of thick bed of autumn leaves on winding path,
and as you walk, reach out to touch the nearby trunks,
the smooth gray bark of mammoth beech
or the alligator-ridges of curving sourwood trees.

And as you walk through purifying winter woods,
don't hesitate to pick some frozen sweet birch twigs,
smell the pleasing wintergreen scent
and place them on your welcoming tongue
to rinse away those heavy words of shame or hate.

On your solitary walk, the beauty of the forest
cascades around you and flows through your soul.
The sights and sounds, the scents and textures,
colors, shapes, and all of nature's harmonies
wash over you, bringing peace and quiet joy.

TRASH DAY

(with thanks to Carl Dennis)

Today, as each year, in April,
we gather on our streets
to beautify our town,
to pick up the year's detritus
blown out of pick-up truck
or tossed unthinkingly from cars.

We six are shown our task:
a street beside the rocky creek.
Young man from nearby rehab center,
two bubbly high school girls,
a mother with her chirping five-year old,
and me, octogenarian, cane in right hand.

The recovering man from rehab
concentrates on battered cans
he pulls from weeds and creek bed,
a variety of brews, in penance,
he remarks, from the frequent times
he tossed cans out his own car window.

The two young women,
dressed in bright, fancy fashion,
are hesitant at first but pull on gloves,
and vie to grab those soggy,
muddy t-shirts, socks, proving
they are more than fashionistas.

How fortunate the five-year old,
who early learns to beautify his world,
who with his mother, delights in finding
cans and bottles, bits of plastic
to drop into the bag she drags behind her.

And me, old man with walking cane,
while bending stiffly down to do his part,
thinks of treasures he has sometimes found:
a Buffalo nickel from the thirties,
one perfect heart-shaped rock,
the joy of serving community,
and two very serviceable right-hand gloves.

CHANGING NATURE

The permanence of nature?
Or always changes?

In those childhood years,
when camping in the nearby woods,
at night, by small campfire,
it was the great unknown,
my first true freedom.

As young adult,
steep, snowy mountain slopes
represented adventure,
nature an obstacle
to be conquered,
proving my worth.

In middle years,
exploring tropical vegetation,
an open book for learning
nature, home to varied human cultures,
became my teacher.

In later years, nature was
a quiet, familiar place,
displaying faithful spring ephemerals
and autumn color,
a welcome haven of calm
in a world of clashing cymbals.

WINTER WONDER

Spring has its awesome floral colors.
We stand amazed by summer's bounty
and by autumn's dazzling foliage.
But let us revel, too, in awe-inspiring winter.

Express your delight at the ephemeral
beauty of rounded mountain peaks,
dusted by hoarfrost overnight,
turned crimson by the rising sun.

When all seems brown in winter's freeze,
give shouts of glee at unexpected sight
of witch hazel blossoms glowing
live and yellow in the frosty air.

On moonless, cloudless winter nights,
let joy ring out, when in the East
the planet Jupiter first shows its face,
accompanied by its faithful moons.

When the north wind's bitter gusts
turn the wind chime's crystal notes
into cheery season's carols,
open wide your ears and sing along.

Make tastebuds dance with winter joy
when sipping holiday season's treats,
like creamy eggnog laced with rich dark rum
or steaming cups of hot Dutch cocoa.

So let's not wait for spring's new life,
for summer's wealth and autumn's fruits.
May our hearts lift up with grateful praise
at signs of winter's awesome gifts.

A CYCLIST'S OBITUARY

He loved his bikes, and today,
on his recumbent bike,
he peddled slowly
into the hills and valleys
of the great beyond.

As a fearless child in Virginia
he clattered everywhere,
often both hands raised high in air,
over oyster shell lanes
and tarry, gravel roads
on his first bicycle,
the red but very rusty Schwinn,
for which his father
had traded an old rowboat.

He later, after numerous falls,
became an expert rider
on a unicycle, once performing
in a small-town circus
behind dancing ponies
and riding slalom in and out
between lumbering elephants.

In the cycle shop,
a brand-new shiny blue
bicycle-built-for-two
once caught his eye,
and he soon found
a strong-legged partner
willing to peddle
from the second seat.

He stood beside his
Peugeot racing bike,

in the welcome shadow
of ancient turreted castles
or on narrow streets where sweet scents
of fresh croissants and chocolate éclairs
wafted from town pastry shops,
as riders by the score
in multi-colored jerseys
(his dreaming of wearing the yellow)
swept toward the finish line
in the Tour de France.

And on the mountain slopes
above Bujumbura
he watched in awe
what he would never dare,
as down the highway
at breakneck speed,
weaving in and out of loaded trucks,
whooshed sturdy bikes
with stacks of crates
filled with empty bottles
or multiple heavy stalks
of bananas, red and yellow.

When thighs and calves then weakened,
and breath came only raspingly,
a cycling friend advised an e-bike
which, with minimal effort,
then carried him high
into the surrounding mountains
to observe once more
spring's ephemerals—
red trillium, trout lilies, and Oconee bells.

And then today, the blinking light
on the back of his recumbent bike
disappeared into the void.

CULINARY SURPRISE

After hours on unpaved, rutted roads
through towering trees and jungle vines,
far from what we thought was civilization,
unsure of finding decent noonday sustenance,
when pleased we were to chance upon
a white-washed, thatched-roof open-air café
beneath a sprawling mango tree,
branches hanging low with shiny purple fruit.

We sat under thatched umbrella roof,
surprised in that forest setting
with red-checked tablecloth
and shiny polished silverware.
Our host, both cook and waiter,
when asked what fare we might enjoy,
announced with smiling voice in perfect French:
"The *plat du jour* is python."

He brought us each a plate
with mammoth thick round python steak
in bubbling aromatic sauce—
"champagne and cream," he said.
And along with it were juicy mango slices,
crisp-fried plantain strips
and glasses filled with bubbly.
With grateful satisfaction, we learned
that taste and beauty and sheer delight,
when eyes and minds are open,
make their surprise appearance.

CHERRY TREE AT WINDOW

Your father planted me, a tender shoot,
the day that you were born, and through
the open window, as I took root,
I heard your hungry wails or tender coos.

My trunk grew strong, my branches leafed,
and blossoms yielded first spring delights
as you began to take those tentative steps,
imitating words, expressing love and joy.

Each fall, by Halloween, my leaves would drop,
and branches waving in the moonlit night
made shadows on your bedroom walls
like evil spirits in your restless youthful dreams.

As you became a man with rich, productive life,
I, too, fulfilled my ordained role: my branches full,
providing tasty fruit, sweet Montmorency cherries,
some within easy reach of open window.

And now, you, once more back in family home,
lying weak and frail and facing shortening days,
remembering dancing shadows and cherries sweet,
gaze through cloudy panes and ponder life well spent.

 I, now with broken branches and pitted trunk,
know that soon a chainsaw end-of-life awaits.
But peace is mine. Like you, I shared my bounty
and lived rich life, our years four-score and ten.

ARRIVAL

The Boeing 707 swept down
over the misty mountains,
tropical jungles steaming below.

The young man stared
from the airplane window
at the immense river below,
almost hoping that the plane
would crash, leaving no survivors.

He had longed for adventure,
but now reality was setting in.
Could he truly face students
in a culture not his own,
in a language he barely knew?
What could he offer?

As he stepped down from the plane,
which hadn't crashed,
and down to the sun-baked runway,
the warm, moist air,
like a wet cotton blanket,
felt too heavy to breathe.

Surely, he thought,
in his naiveté, the miasmic air
was filled with pathogens:
all those feared tropical diseases,
malaria, schistosomiasis,
sleeping sickness, dengue fever.
How would he survive two years?

SOUPE À L'OIGNON

After the theater in Paris, near midnight we'd go,
to savor onion soup in a corner café.
They'd bring out hot bowls with their faces aglow,
and they'd give us this recipe to carry away:

Choose some fat onions, maybe three pounds,
You will weep as you chop and you slice,
But you can muffle the sounds.
Sauté them in butter until they smell nice.

Add one full cup of dry white wine
Plus several ounces of good Spanish sherry.
Some all-purpose flour mixed in will be fine.
As the mixture gets thicker, begin to make merry.

Then in your big stew crock,
As the warm smells grow heady,
Pour in two quarts of beef stock.
Boil for ten minutes till ready.

Now fill up some ramekins to the top, if you please,
And cover each top with some toasted French bread.
Then sprinkle it all with fresh Gruyère cheese,
Or you might prefer Parmesan and use it instead.

Don't forget flavor with pepper and salt,
Place under the broiler and turn up the heat.
When the cheese gets all crusty, remove without fault,
Then sit down at the table and savor the treat.

A SPRING BLESSING

As our second year reaches fulfillment,
May your eyes retain their sparkle.

As the April breeze sets azalea blooms aquiver,
May the joy of springtime fill your heart.

As the red-tailed hawk soars along our mountain peaks,
May your spirit rise to meet the best in humanity.

As the season's showers call forth flowers,
May your creative juices well up and overflow.

As the full moon rises, golden through the oaks,
May gratitude swell and crest.

As blueberry blossoms open white and pink,
May the prospect of muffins caress your tastebuds.

As our libraries reopen their doors,
May you find books to nourish your mind.

As we display our all too human foibles,
May your smile and sense of humor remain intact.

And above all, as we embark together on our year three,
May you experience constant love and support.

ENDURANCE

On the rocky outcrop,
no place for rich dark loam,
the sun beats down
each scorching day
on the Bristlecone Pine
inching upward
despite all odds.

Through the pavement
outside our front door,
with little space for roots
and no protective mulch
fighting the sun's rays
through rainless August days,
the scraggly tomato plant
clings to life.

Enduring nurses' pokes and probes,
support by cane and crutch,
my human body fights through pain,
draws sustenance not yet from steak and bread
but thankfully at least
from fruit and soup.
My frame stands tall
and takes firm trial steps.

Despite all hardships,
when all around seems gray and grim,
with roots in rocks and concrete
or pain in all extremities,
fresh cones appear on the Bristlecone,
yellow fruit thrives on thin green stalks,
and human courage still stays strong.

LUCKY LUKE

The fearsome Dalton brothers
gave my daughter nightmares,
and Lucky Luke, who could draw
faster than his shadow,
rode through my son's Wild West
childhood dreams on his horse,
Jolly Jumper.

If only, you my daughter,
with your brother,
could see them now:
horse, the brothers Dalton,
and Lucky Luke himself,
staring out of windows
in Angoulême.

www.ingramcontent.com/pod-product-compliance
Lightning Source LLC
Chambersburg PA
CBHW070632030426
42337CB00020B/3987